MAVERICK

AN UNAUTHORIZED COLLECTION OF WISDOM FROM

JOHN McCAIN

THE SHERIFF OF THE SENATE

MARY ZAIA

Castle Point Books
New York

www.castlepointbooks.com
www.stmartins.com

The Castle Point Books trademark is owned by Castle Point Publications, LLC.
Castle Point books are published and distributed by St. Martin's Press.

ISBN 978-1-250-20018-1
ISBN 978-1-250-20019-8 (e-book)

Design by Katie Jennings Campbell
Production by Tara Long
Cover illustration by Kimma Parish

Our books may be purchased in bulk for promotional, educational,
or business use. Please contact your local bookseller or the
Macmillan Corporate and Premium Sales Department at 1-800-221-7945,
extension 5442, or by e-mail at MacmillanSpecialMarkets@macmillan.com.

First Edition

10 9 8 7 6 5 4 3 2 1

CONTENTS

THE MAKING OF A
MAVERICK

WHO WOULD HAVE THOUGHT that a man who graduated fifth from the bottom of his class at the Naval Academy would go on to become a POW hero and the Republican nominee for president [in 2008]? Anyone who ever met John McCain and his maverick spirit!

A six-term senator from Arizona, McCain was outspoken even from the start of his political career. He continued to raise his voice over decades in office on many issues, including foreign policy, human rights, climate change, campaign finance reform, and pork-barrel spending. Rather than towing the line, he quickly earned a reputation as a straight shooter not afraid to challenge his own party. In 1983, he called for the withdrawal of U.S. Marines from Lebanon. Decades later, he challenged President Trump and Republican attempts to repeal the Affordable Care Act. He's respected for crossing political divides and lauding the achievements of men and women "across the aisle." [Consider his bromance with Joe Biden.]

The secret to his success, according to John: growing up surrounded by people who placed a high value on character and honor. [Both McCain's father and paternal grandfather rose to four-star admirals.] McCain has also credited how much he learned from the most challenging experiences of his life—including surviving $5\frac{1}{2}$ years [$3\frac{1}{2}$ of those in solitary confinement] as a POW in Vietnam. McCain earned the Silver Star, Bronze Star, Purple Heart, and Distinguished Flying Cross. But he said the greatest prizes of his service were the bonds formed between him and his fellow POWs.

Even after his diagnosis of aggressive brain cancer, McCain continued working between treatments, relying on thankfulness for each day and service to his country to keep him strong. Rarely speechless, McCain responded to his prognosis, "I just said, 'I understand. Now we're going to do what we can, get the best doctors we can find, and do the best we can.' And at the same time celebrate with gratitude a life well-lived." Let McCain's words of wisdom inspire you to call out the truth, invest yourself in the fight to keep American ideals alive, bridge divisions, and live a life of honorable service to country and others.

FOR
LOVE OF
COUNTRY

In prison, I fell in love with my country. I had loved her before then, but like most young people, my affection was little more than a simple appreciation for the comforts and privileges most Americans enjoyed and took for granted. It wasn't until I had lost America for a time that I realized how much I loved her.

Faith of My Fathers: A Family Memoir

What a privilege it is to serve this **BIG, BOISTEROUS, BRAWLING, INTEMPERATE, STRIVING, DARING, BEAUTIFUL, BOUNTIFUL, BRAVE, MAGNIFICENT** country.

Remarks at the 2017 Liberty Medal Ceremony,
October 16, 2017

Americans are very frustrated, and they have every right to be. We've wasted a lot of our most precious treasure, which is American lives.

Announcing his entry into the 2008 U.S. presidential race, on *Late Show with David Letterman*, February 2007

I BELIEVE IN AMERICANS.

We're capable of better. I've seen it. We're hopeful, compassionate people.

Address to Naval Academy graduates,
October 30, 2017

Sacrifices made by veterans deserve to be memorialized in something more lasting than marble or bronze, or in the fleeting effect of a politician's speeches.

Commemorating Veterans Day,
November 10, 2017

TO FEAR THE WORLD we have organized and led for three-quarters of a century…for the sake of some half-baked, spurious nationalism cooked up by people who would rather find scapegoats than solve problems is as unpatriotic as an attachment to any other tired dogma of the past that Americans consigned to the ash heap of history.

Remarks at the 2017 Liberty Medal Ceremony,
October 16, 2017

I call on all Americans...

to not despair of our present difficulties but to believe always in the promise and greatness of America, because nothing is inevitable here.

Concession speech, November 8, 2008

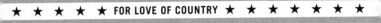
I BELIEVE DEEPLY IN THE GREATNESS OF AMERICA'S DESTINY AND IN THE GOODNESS OF OUR CAUSE.

Speech declaring candidacy for the
Republican presidential nomination,
September 28, 1999

I've seen Americans make sacrifices for our country and her causes and for people who were strangers to them but for our common humanity, **SACRIFICES THAT WERE MUCH HARDER THAN THE SERVICE ASKED OF ME.**

Address to Ohio Wesleyan University,
May 11, 1996

Ultimately, America's greatest strength comes from the values of our society… **our commitment to truth over falsehood,** fairness over injustice, **freedom over oppression,** and the immortal spirit of humankind.

Remarks at the U.S. Studies Center
in Sydney, Australia, May 30, 2017

With all our flaws, all our mistakes,
with all the frailties of human nature
as much on display as our virtues, with
all the rancor and anger of our politics,
WE ARE BLESSED.

Remarks at the 2017 Liberty Medal Ceremony,
October 16, 2017

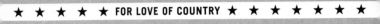

BUT AS BLESSED AS WE ARE,

no nation complacent in its greatness can long sustain it.

Address at Jacksonville, Florida,
April 3, 2008

We are living in the land of the free...

the land where a person can escape the consequences of a self-centered youth and know the satisfaction of sacrificing for an ideal, the land where you can go from aimless rebellion to a noble cause, and from the bottom of your class to your party's nomination for president.

Remarks at the 2017 Liberty Medal Ceremony,
October 16, 2017

WE ARE
AMERICANS FIRST,
AMERICANS LAST,
AND AMERICANS
ALWAYS.

Speech at the Republican National Convention,
August 30, 2004

Today, I was a candidate for the highest office in the country I love so much. And tonight, I remain her servant. That is blessing enough for anyone.

Concession speech, November 8, 2008

Among the few compensations of old age is the acuity of hindsight. I see now that I was part of something important...along for the ride as America made the future better than the past.

Remarks at the 2017 Liberty Medal Ceremony,
October 16, 2017

I OWE AMERICA MORE THAN SHE HAS EVER OWED ME.

Speech declaring candidacy for
the Republican presidential nomination,
September 28, 1999

THE
GOOD FIGHT

Nothing in life is more liberating than to fight for a cause larger than yourself, something that encompasses you but is not defined by your existence alone.

Faith of My Fathers: A Family Memoir

I don't mind a good fight. For reasons known only to God, I've had quite a few tough ones in my life. But I learned an important lesson along the way:

IN THE END, IT MATTERS LESS THAT YOU CAN FIGHT. WHAT YOU FIGHT FOR IS THE REAL TEST.

Speech at the Republican National Convention,
September 4, 2008

THE ARC OF HISTORY DOES NOT BEND INEVITABLY TOWARD JUSTICE. AS ALWAYS, THAT IS UP TO US.

Remarks at the U.S. Studies Center
in Sydney, Australia, May 30, 2017

I know what courage looks like. I know what it can do. **I know its different expressions.** I think I know what it costs.

Why Courage Matters

IN AMERICA, we change things that need to be changed. Each generation makes its contribution to our greatness.

Speech at the Republican National Convention,
September 4, 2008

Americans never quit.
We never surrender.
We never hide
from history.
We make history.

Concession speech, November 8, 2008

Courage is not
the absence of fear
**BUT THE CAPACITY
TO ACT DESPITE
OUR FEARS.**

Why Courage Matters

I've seen America become a more just and prosperous country, coming ever closer to the ideals set down by our founders. **I've seen America organize and lead an international order based on liberty, mutual security, free markets, and the rule of law that liberated millions upon millions from tyranny and poverty.** But we need only look back upon my own lifetime to understand how hard-fought those victories were.

Address to Naval Academy graduates,
October 30, 2017

We can admire virtue and abhor corruption sincerely, **but without courage we are corruptible.**

Why Courage Matters

IT IS NO EASY THING BEING TRULY BRAVE.

Why Courage Matters

I HAVE AN ACUTE, MUCH TOO ACUTE, SENSITIVITY TO ABUSES OF AUTHORITY.

Worth the Fighting For

If we take up the mantle of reviving the universal liberal values and our national political institutions,

WE CAN CHOOSE ORDER OVER CHAOS.

"Words That Matter: Chaos," Medium, December 7, 2017

WE SHOULD ASPIRE TO BE **BRAVE, COMPASSIONATE,** AND **EXTRAORDINARY** WHEN FACING DANGER.

"We Draw Upon the Spirit of the
Granite Mountain Hotshots,"
Medium, June 30, 2017

I'm going to fight with every ounce of strength I have, BUT I'M GOING TO KEEP FIGHTING CLEAN, I'M GOING TO KEEP FIGHTING FAIR, AND I'M GOING TO KEEP FIGHTING THE BATTLE OF IDEAS.

Remarks following the South Carolina primary,
February 19, 2000

At least with this fight,
I KNOW
THE ENEMY.

On battling cancer versus surviving as a POW,
interview with C-SPAN, October 18, 2017

There's never been a problem Americans couldn't solve. We are the world's leaders, and leaders don't fear change.

Speech at Carnegie Mellon University,
April 15, 2008

I AM COUNTING ON YOU TO KEEP THE FAITH, AND NEVER GIVE UP... never, ever stop fighting for all that is good, and just, and decent about our world, and each other.

Letter to Munich Security Conference,
delivered February 17, 2018

STRAIGHT TALK

Senator Obama,
I'm not President Bush.

If you want to run against President Bush, you should have run four years ago.

Final U.S. TV presidential debate,
October 15, 2008

I CLAIM NO MORAL SUPERIORITY OVER DONALD TRUMP. I have a long and well-known public and private record for which I will have to answer at the Final Judgment.... I challenge the nominee to set the example for what our country can and should represent.

Statement regarding Donald Trump's comments about Khizr and Ghazala Khan, the parents of U.S. Army Captain Humayun Khan, who was killed in Iraq, August 1, 2016

Whether or not we are of the same party, we are not the president's subordinates.

WE ARE HIS EQUAL!

Remarks on Senate floor,
July 25, 2017

…when I hear the Senate referred to as the world's greatest deliberative body. I'm not sure we can claim that distinction with a straight face today.

Remarks on Senate floor,
July 25, 2017

WAR IS WRETCHED BEYOND DESCRIPTION, and only a fool or a fraud could sentimentalize its cruel reality.

Speech to American Red Cross,
May 1999

I DON'T BLAME THEM.
WHEN YOU ARE IN A WAR
AND YOU ARE CAPTURED
BY THE ENEMY, YOU CAN'T
EXPECT TO HAVE TEA.

On his POW captors, interview with C-SPAN,
October 18, 2017

How did we end up here? Why do many Americans ignore our moral and historical knowledge?

Address to Naval Academy graduates,
October 30, 2017

LEADERSHIP
IS BOTH BURDEN
AND PRIVILEGE.

Address to Ohio Wesleyan University,
May 11, 1996

The Republican Party I know and love is the party of Abraham Lincoln, Theodore Roosevelt, Dwight D. Eisenhower, and Ronald Reagan.

Statement released August 1, 2016

We spent $3 million to study the DNA of bears in Montana. I don't know if that was a paternity issue or a criminal issue.

On wasteful congressional spending, at Saddleback Church Forum, August 2008

HOW DO WE EXPLAIN TO AMERICANS who are risking their lives for us that we could not summon the courage to take some hard votes? How do we explain that we could not come together and work together when it mattered most?

"On Final Passage of the National Defense Authorization Act," Medium, September 18, 2017

I'M OLDER THAN DIRT AND HAVE MORE SCARS THAN FRANKENSTEIN,

BUT I'VE LEARNED A FEW THINGS ALONG THE WAY.

Common response when asked about his age

Stop listening to
the bombastic
loudmouths on the
radio and television
and the Internet....
**Our incapacity is
their livelihood.**

Remarks on Senate floor,
July 25, 2017

Believe in our country, love our founding truths, honor the sacrifice of our soldiers, be a good citizen, and fly on the damn airplane. **That's all I can offer in the way of instruction to people who might feel incapacitated by the threat of terrorism.**

Why Courage Matters

I'm an independent-minded, well-intentioned public servant to some. And to others, I'm a self-styled, self-righteous, maverick pain in the ass.

Worth the Fighting For

I've had so many people say such nice things about me recently that I think some of you must have me confused with someone else.

Remarks on Senate floor, July 25, 2017

AMERICAN POPULAR CULTURE
ADMITS FEW SENIOR CITIZENS
TO ITS RANKS OF CELEBRATED
NONCONFORMISTS. We lack the
glamorous carelessness of youth
and risk becoming parodies of
our younger selves.

Worth the Fighting For

BRIDGING DIVIDES

We have to remind our sons and daughters that we became the most powerful nation on earth by tearing down walls, not building them.

Address to Naval Academy graduates,
October 30, 2017

Compromise and working across the aisle have become political liabilities, when they were meant to define our legislative process.

"Words That Matter: Chaos," Medium,
December 7, 2017

Whatever the outcome next month, **Senator Obama has achieved a great thing** for himself and for his country and I congratulate him.

Remarks at the Al Smith Dinner
in New York City, October 16, 2008

But that he managed to do so by inspiring the hopes of so many millions of Americans who had once wrongly believed that they had little at stake or little influence in the election of an American president is something I deeply admire and commend him for achieving.

Speaking of Barack Obama in concession speech, November 8, 2008

Thank you @joebiden & the entire Biden family for serving as an example & source of strength for my own family.

@SenJohnMcCain Twitter, December 13, 2017

The most revered members of this institution accepted the **necessity of compromise** in order to make incremental progress on solving America's problems and to defend her from her adversaries.

Remarks on Senate floor, July 25, 2017

I hope we can again rely on humility, **on our need to cooperate,** on our dependence on each other to learn how to trust each other.

Remarks on Senate floor, July 25, 2017

We are asleep in our echo chambers, where our views are always affirmed and information that contradicts them is always fake. We are asleep in our polarized politics, which exaggerates our differences, looks for scapegoats instead of answers, and insists we get all our way all the time from a system of government based on compromise, principled cooperation and restraint....

IT'S TIME TO WAKE UP.

Address to Naval Academy graduates,
October 30, 2017

It shouldn't be beyond us to refrain from substituting character assassination and mean-spiritedness **for spirited debate.**

"On Vice President Joe Biden and Civility,"
Medium, June 7, 2016

We have nothing to fear from each other. WE ARE ARGUING OVER THE MEANS TO BETTER SECURE OUR FREEDOM AND PROMOTE THE GENERAL WELFARE. BUT IT SHOULD REMAIN AN ARGUMENT AMONG FRIENDS WHO SHARE AN UNSHAKEN BELIEF IN OUR GREAT CAUSE, AND IN THE GOODNESS OF EACH OTHER.

Speech at the Republican National Convention,
August 30, 2004

Instead of rejecting good ideas because we didn't think of them first, **LET'S USE THE BEST IDEAS FROM BOTH SIDES.** Instead of fighting over who gets the credit, **LET'S TRY SHARING IT.**

Speech at the Republican National Convention,
September 4, 2008

I URGE ALL AMERICANS...

to bridge our differences, and help restore our prosperity, defend our security in a dangerous world, and leave our children and grandchildren a stronger, better country than we inherited.

Concession speech, November 8, 2008

We live in a land made of ideals, not blood and soil. We are the custodians of those ideals at home, and their champion abroad.

Remarks at the 2017 Liberty Medal Ceremony,
October 16, 2017

Merely preventing your political opponents from doing what they **want** isn't the most inspiring work.

Remarks on Senate floor, July 25, 2017

I AM A UNITER, NOT A DIVIDER.

Remarks following the South Carolina primary,
February 19, 2000

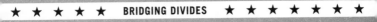

I WILL WORK WITH ANYONE

who sincerely wants to get this country moving again.

Speech at the Greater Columbus Convention Center in Ohio, May 15, 2008

In so many ways, WE NEED TO MAKE A CLEAN BREAK FROM THE WORST EXCESSES OF BOTH POLITICAL PARTIES.

Speech at Carnegie Mellon University,
April 15, 2008

We are fellow Americans and fellow human beings, who possess equal dignity and rights, and in the end, our shared identity is so much more important than our differences.

"On Vice President Joe Biden and Civility," Medium,
June 7, 2016

WE HAVE TO FIGHT against propaganda and crackpot conspiracy theories.
WE HAVE TO FIGHT isolationism, protectionism, and nativism.
WE HAVE TO DEFEAT those who would worsen our divisions.

Address to Naval Academy graduates,
October 30, 2017

THE WORLD
I KNOW

Who could have imagined in the depths of the Cold War that a collapsing Soviet Union—still a nuclear superpower—would peacefully accede to the reunification of Germany, or to the independence of all of its satellite states? **AND YET IT HAPPENED.**

Address to Naval Academy graduates,
October 30, 2017

The international order
we helped build from the
ashes of world war, and
that we defend to this day,
**has liberated more people
from tyranny and poverty**
than ever before in history.

Remarks at the 2017 Liberty Medal Ceremony,
October 16, 2017

How do we make sense of the human capacity for such evil?

After Auschwitz, mankind looked different.

Address to Naval Academy graduates,
October 30, 2017

HOWEVER HEADY THE
APPEAL OF A CALL TO ARMS,
HOWEVER JUST THE CAUSE,
WE SHOULD STILL SHED A
TEAR FOR ALL THAT IS LOST
WHEN WAR CLAIMS ITS
WAGES FROM US.

Address at Jacksonville, Florida,
April 3, 2008

That is a black mark on this country,

asking the lowest-income level to fight for us while the wealthiest stayed home.

On Vietnam, interview with C-SPAN,
October 18, 2017

I ARGUED THEN,
AND I ARGUE NOW,

THAT IT WAS WRONG TO USE THESE

METHODS, THAT IT UNDERMINED OUR

SECURITY INTERESTS, AND THAT IT

CONTRADICTED THE IDEALS THAT DEFINE

US AND WHICH WE HAVE SACRIFICED

MUCH TO DEFEND.

"There Can Be No Justification for Torture," Medium,
November 15, 2017

At this time of increasing uncertainty and growing security challenges, **it is imperative that we reassert the United States' commitment to our human rights obligations,** and ask other countries to join us in reaffirming the centrality of human rights as the cornerstone of peace and security.

From letter to the president cowritten with
Senator Ben Cardin (D-MD), December 8, 2017

Our government has a responsibility to defend our borders, but we must do so in a way that makes us safer and **upholds all that is decent and exceptional about our nation.**

Statement with Lindsay Graham [R-SC] on
Executive Order on Immigration, January 29, 2017

There is no greater threat to our freedoms than attacks on our ability to choose our own leaders free from foreign interference.

"Sending a Message to Vladimir Putin," Medium,
June 7, 2017

And so, we must take our own side in this fight—

NOT AS REPUBLICANS,
NOT AS DEMOCRATS,
BUT AS AMERICANS.

It's time to respond to Russia's attack on American democracy with strength, with resolve, with common purpose, and with action.

"Sending a Message to Vladimir Putin," Medium,
June 7, 2017

I HATE THE PRESS...

BUT THE FACT IS WE NEED YOU. WE NEED A FREE PRESS. WE MUST HAVE IT. IT'S VITAL.

Statement at the 53rd Munich Security
Conference in Munich, Germany, February 17, 2017

@pressfreedom's annual report shows record # of journalists imprisoned worldwide in 2017, including 21 on "fake news" charges. @POTUS must understand his harmful rhetoric only empowers repressive regimes to jail reporters & silence the truth.

@SenJohnMcCain Twitter,
December 13, 2017

OUR TROOPS HAVE FOUGHT BRAVELY AND HONORABLY, but too often, it seemed as if they were doing so with one hand tied behind their back.

"Will the President's New Strategy Turn the Tide in Afghanistan?" Medium, October 3, 2017

The U.S. stands with the brave protesters who yearn for freedom,
peace, and an end to corruption in Iran.

@SenJohnMcCain Twitter,
December 30, 2017

HOW MUCH DAMAGE WILL HAVE BEEN DONE

BEFORE WE ACT?

On global warming, interview
with *The New Yorker*, 2003

The times we live in are alternately **derided for their failings** and **romanticized for their emerging opportunities.**

Address to Ohio Wesleyan University,
May 11, 1996

It is our destiny to seize this opportunity

to build a safer, freer, and more prosperous nation and a world free of...tyranny.

Speech declaring candidacy for the Republican presidential nomination, September 28, 1999

SOMETHING GREATER

GLORY belongs to the act of being constant to something greater than yourself, **to a cause, to your principles,** to the people on whom you rely and who rely on you.

Address at Jacksonville, Florida,
April 3, 2008

As a prisoner of war, I learned that
a shared purpose did not claim
my identity. On the contrary, it
enlarged my sense of myself. I have
the example of many brave men
to thank for that discovery, all of
them proud of their singularity,
but faithful to the same cause.

Faith of My Fathers: A Family Memoir

I've been repaid a thousand times over

with adventures, with good company, and with the satisfaction of serving something more important than myself, of being a bit player in the extraordinary story of America.

Remarks at the 2017 Liberty Medal Ceremony,
October 16, 2017

I'm not running for president to be somebody, but to do something; to do the hard but necessary things, not the easy and needless things.

Announcement for his 2008 presidential bid,
April 25, 2007

The problem solving
our system does make
possible, the fitful progress
it produces, and the liberty
and justice it preserves,
**IS A MAGNIFICENT
ACHIEVEMENT.**

Remarks on Senate floor,
July 25, 2017

With all its suffering and dangers, the world still looks to THE EXAMPLE AND LEADERSHIP OF AMERICA to become, another, better place.

Remarks at the 2017 Liberty Medal Ceremony,
October 16, 2017

WHAT OUR ENEMIES HAVE SOUGHT
TO DESTROY IS BEYOND THEIR REACH.

IT CANNOT BE TAKEN
FROM US. IT CAN ONLY
BE SURRENDERED.

Speech at the Republican National Convention,
August 30, 2004

Like most people of my age, I feel a longing for what is lost and cannot be restored. But...something better can endure, and endure until our last moment on earth. And that is the honor we earn and the love we give if at a moment in our lives we sacrifice for something greater than self-interest.

Address to Ohio Wesleyan University,
May 11, 1996

At its core, the economy isn't the sum of an array of bewildering statistics.... It's about the aspirations of the American people to build a better life for their families;

DREAMS THAT BEGIN WITH A JOB.

Speech before the League of American Latin Citizens, July 7, 2008

In our free society, it is left to each one of us to make our own way in the world—and our jobs, businesses, savings, pensions, farms, and homes are the work of years. Take these away and you are diminishing a lot more than the GDP, or the final tally on the Big Board on Wall Street. Take these away, and a million dreams are undone.

Speech at Carnegie Mellon University,
April 15, 2008

This is no time to despair—for on our side we have the cause of truth, and right, and justice. **This is a time to trust each other, rely on each other, roll up our sleeves together,** and work even harder on behalf of the values, and the world order, and the way of life that we all hold dear.

Remarks at the 2017 Brussels Forum,
March 25, 2017

Even in the worst of times (and they come for most of us) you'll know that to serve this country is to serve its ideals—the ideals that consider every child on earth as made in the image of God and **ENDOWED WITH DIGNITY AND THE RIGHTS TO LIFE, LIBERTY, AND THE PURSUIT OF HAPPINESS.**

Address to Naval Academy graduates,
October 30, 2017

We have to love our freedom, not just for the material benefits it provides, not just for the autonomy it guarantees us, **but for the goodness it makes possible.**

Speech at the Republican National Convention,
August 30, 2004

My friends, if you find faults with our country, make it a better one. If you're disappointed with the mistakes of government, join its ranks and work to correct them. Enlist in our Armed Forces. **Become a teacher.** Enter the ministry. **Run for public office.** Feed a hungry child. **Teach an illiterate adult to read.** Comfort the afflicted. **Defend the rights of the oppressed.**

Speech at the Republican National Convention,
September 4, 2008

I learned in Vietnam how short a distance separates the individualist from the egotist and how neither can match

THE STRENGTH OF A COMMUNITY UNITED TO SERVE A CAUSE GREATER THAN SELF-INTEREST.

Worth the Fighting For

We have much to do in this historically pivotal era of great change and challenge, to ensure, as every preceding American generation has, **that the country we leave our children is even better than the one we inherited.**

Address at Jacksonville, Florida,
April 3, 2008

The passive life
is not worth forgoing the
satisfaction of knowing that
you chose to employ all
the blessings God bestowed
on you to **leaving the
world a little better for
your presence in it.**

Address to Ohio Wesleyan University,
May 11, 1996

WITH HARD WORK, STRONG FAITH, AND A LITTLE COURAGE, GREAT THINGS ARE ALWAYS WITHIN OUR REACH.

Speech at the Republican National Convention,
September 4, 2008

I've never lived a day, in good times or bad, that I didn't thank God for the privilege.

Speech at the Republican National Convention,
September 4, 2008

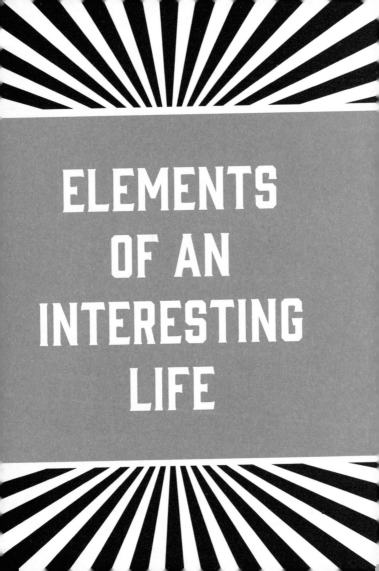

ELEMENTS
OF AN
INTERESTING
LIFE

Our family lived on the move, rooted not in a location, but in the culture of the Navy.
I learned from my mother not just to take the constant disruptions in stride, but welcome them as elements of an interesting life.

Faith of My Fathers: A Family Memoir

I would not want to be again the boy I once was... unless I could keep the knowledge I have acquired with experience while enjoying the strength and enthusiasm of youth.

Address to Ohio Wesleyan University,
May 11, 1996

It is a surpassing irony of war, for all the horrors and heroism it occasions, it provides the soldier with every conceivable human experience. Experiences that usually take a lifetime to know are all felt, and felt intensely, in one brief passage of life.

Address at Jacksonville, Florida,
April 3, 2008

I was blessed by misfortune.... I was blessed because I served in the company of heroes and I witnessed a thousand acts of courage, and compassion, and love.

Speech at the Republican National Convention,
September 4, 2008

When I had reached the limit of my endurance... I became dependent on others to a greater extent than I had ever been before. **And I am a better man for it.**

Address at Jacksonville, Florida,
April 3, 2008

THE JOY OF MY LIFE

WAS THE BONDS THAT WERE FORGED BETWEEN ME AND MY FELLOW POWs.

Interview on *60 Minutes*,
September 24, 2017

I DON'T BELIEVE IN DESTINY.

We are not born to become one thing or another, left to follow helplessly a course that was charted for us by some unseen hand, a mysterious alignment of the stars that pulls us in a certain direction, bestowing happiness on some and misfortune on others.

Character Is Destiny

I believe in evolution.
But I also believe,
when I hike the Grand
Canyon and see it at
sunset, that the hand
of God is there also.

Simi Valley Republican Debate,
May 3, 2007

If I took offense at everybody who has said something about me, or disparaged me or something like that—

LIFE IS TOO SHORT. YOU'VE GOTTA MOVE ON.

Interview on *60 Minutes*,
September 24, 2017

I am almost constantly surrounded by people, **AND I WOULD NOT HAVE IT ANY OTHER WAY.**

Worth the Fighting For

For most people, life is long enough, and varied enough to account for occasional mistakes and failures.

Address to Ohio Wesleyan University,
May 11, 1996

I WON'T SPEND A MOMENT OF THE FUTURE regretting what might have been.

Concession speech, November 8, 2008

I left war behind me, and never let the worst of it encumber my progress.

Faith of My Fathers: A Family Memoir

YOU'VE GOTTA HAVE JOY.

Interview with CNN,
September 10, 2017

I have brought to [elected office] the same idiosyncrasies that marked my career in uniform, chief among them my desire to be my own man, to serve, to the greatest extent possible, on my own terms.

Worth the Fighting For

We must know ourselves,

our own strengths and weaknesses,
and how best to employ the former
and compensate for the latter.

Hard Call

I'M VERY HAPPY WITH MY LIFE AND WHAT I'VE BEEN ABLE TO DO.

Interview with CNN, September 10, 2017

NOTHING ATTRACTS THE HUMAN SPIRIT MORE THAN THE APPRECIATION THAT THERE REMAINS KNOWLEDGE AND EXPERIENCES TO BE ACQUIRED.

Address to Ohio Wesleyan University,
May 11, 1996

There are a great many **SECOND, THIRD,** and **FOURTH** acts for Americans in all walks of life.

Address to Ohio Wesleyan University,
May 11, 1996

CHARACTER & HONOR

It is your character, **and your character alone,** that will make your life happy or unhappy.

Character Is Destiny

If we spent more time searching for our courage and less time imagining the changes it might work in our personalities, **we would probably die with fewer regrets.**

Why Courage Matters

I was raised in the concept and belief that **DUTY, HONOR, COUNTRY** is the lodestar for the behavior that we have to exhibit every single day.

Interview on *60 Minutes*,
September 24, 2017

Children rarely appreciate
fully the sacrifices their
parents make, no matter
how much we remind them.
That's human nature.

Why Courage Matters

THAT'S THE ESSENCE OF REAL HUMILITY....

IT'S REALIZING THAT YOU HAVE AS MUCH DIGNITY IN THE EYES OF GOD AS ANYONE ELSE, BUT NOT ONE BIT MORE.

"On Vice President Joe Biden and Civility,"
Medium, June 7, 2016

I FEAR MANY THINGS,

BUT ONLY FEW THINGS MORE THAN APPEARING RIDICULOUS.

Worth the Fighting For

Your character is not tested on occasions of public scrutiny or acclaim. It is not tested in moments when the object of your actions is the regard of another. Your character is what you are to yourself, not what you pretend to be to yourself or others.

Address to Ohio Wesleyan University,
May 11, 1996

I have spent time in the company of heroes. I was raised by them, **served with them,** was taught to revere them through instruction on the tradition of martial courage.

Why Courage Matters

I HAVE WATCHED MEN SUFFER THE ANGUISH OF IMPRISONMENT, defy appalling human cruelty until further resistance is impossible, break for a moment, then recover inhuman strength to defy their enemies once more.

Address to the Naval Academy,
May 26, 1993

I have long believed these—
**awareness, foresight, timing,
confidence, humility,** and
inspiration—are the qualities
typically represented in the best
decisions and in the characters
of those who make them.

Hard Call

There are many people in Congress, and in the rest of government, who are SMARTER, WISER, and MORE CAPABLE than I am. To be in their company is a privilege and a first-rate education.

Worth the Fighting For

I will not take the **low road** to the **highest office** in this land. I want the presidency in the **best way**, not the **worst way**.

Remarks following the South Carolina primary, February 19, 2000

ALTHOUGH HUMAN BEINGS OFTEN ATTEMPT SELF-DELUSION, WE CANNOT FOREVER HIDE THE TRUTH ABOUT OURSELVES FROM OURSELVES.

Address to Ohio Wesleyan University,
May 11, 1996

PERHAPS THE OLDER WE ARE, AND THE MORE FIXED OUR SHORTCOMINGS ARE, **the more we can use inspiration to encourage our escape from the restraints of our deficiencies.**

Character Is Destiny

I arrived a rebel without a cause, and left much the same. But I would discover that a sense of honor had been imparted to me here that would speak to me in the darkest hours.

Address to Naval Academy graduates,
October 30, 2017

I will never dishonor the
nation I love or myself
by letting ambition
overcome principle.
NEVER. NEVER. NEVER.

Remarks following the South Carolina primary,
February 19, 2000

I celebrate what a guy who stood fifth from the bottom of his class at the Naval Academy has been able to do. **Every night when I go to sleep, I am just filled with gratitude.**

Interview on *60 Minutes*,
September 24, 2017

No one of good character leaves behind a wasted life—

whether they die in obscurity or renown.

Address to Ohio Wesleyan University,
May 11, 1996

A LIFE'S DURATION IS NOT ITS ONLY MEASURE.

Remarks at a memorial service honoring
fallen USS *John S. McCain* sailors,
October 30, 2017

He served his country,

and not always right—made a lot of mistakes, made a lot of errors—**but served his country, and I hope we could add, honorably.**

When asked how he wanted to be remembered, interview with CNN, September 10, 2017

I have been granted a place, albeit a very small one, in American history, and I have been permitted, warts and all, to spend my entire life in the service of my country.

LUCKY ME.

Worth the Fighting For